LET'S GO
2nd Edition
to the English World
1

Phonics

Single Letters

CONTENTS

Appendix Phonics Words
Readers
Flashcards
Stickers

Workbook

The Alphabet

Aa		Bb	
Cc		Dd	
Ee		Ff	
Gg		Hh	
Ii		Jj	
Kk		Ll	

Mm		Nn	
Oo		Pp	
Qq		Rr	
Ss		Tt	
Uu		Vv	
Ww		Xx	
Yy		Zz	

How to Hold a Pencil

Hold the pencil gently with your **1** index finger and **2** thumb.

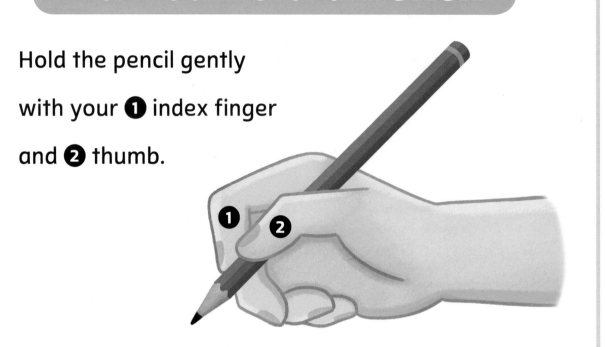

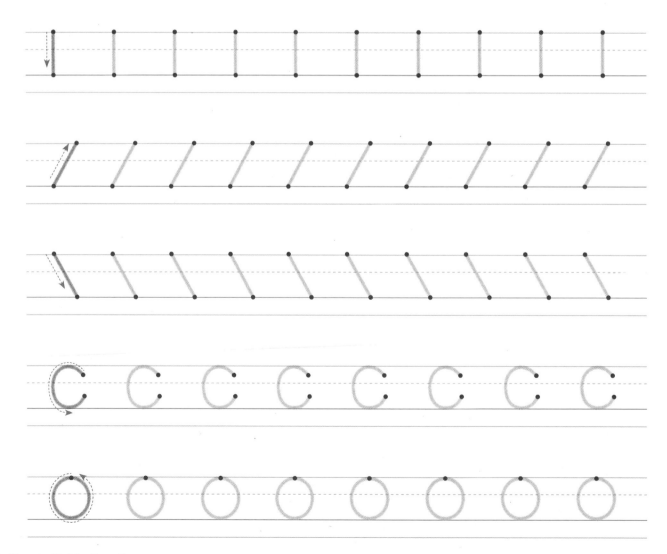

Trace the Letters

Aa Bb Cc Dd

Ee Ff Gg Hh

Ii Jj Kk Ll

Mm Nn Oo Pp

Qq Rr Ss Tt

Uu Vv Ww Xx

Yy Zz

Aa, Bb, Cc

● **Listen and repeat.** 03

 Aa

 Bb

Cc

A **Point and chant.** 04

Aa Bb Cc

B Say and trace.

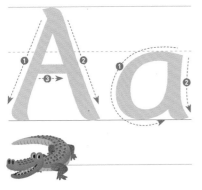

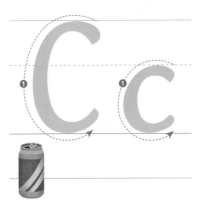

A A A

B B B

C C C

a a a

b b b

c c c

C Circle and match.

1.
A | b | ⓐ | c

2.
B | a | b | c

3.
C | c | b | a

A Listen and color.

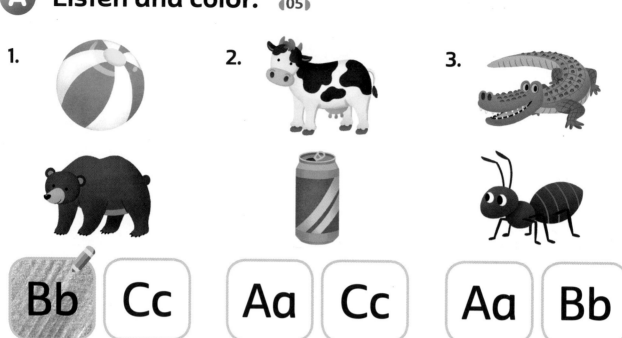

1.

Bb   Cc

2.

Aa   Cc

3.

Aa   Bb

B Look and stick.

1.   **b**

2.   sticker

3.   sticker

4.   sticker

5.   sticker

C **Listen, connect and read.** 06

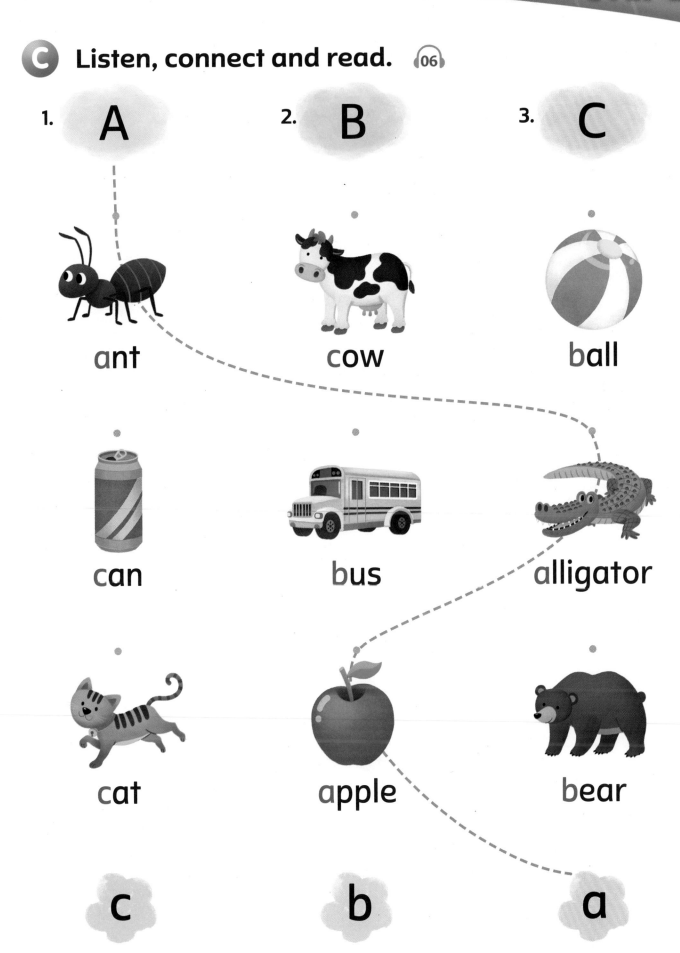

1. A
2. B
3. C

ant

cow

ball

can

bus

alligator

cat

apple

bear

c

b

a

● **Let's read together.** 07

I'm on the apple.
I'm in the bus.
I'm in the alligator.

Thank you, bear!

Sight Words

I'm   on   the   in

Writing Time

● **Listen and write.** (08)

1.

alligator

lligator

2.

ant

nt

3.

apple

pple

4.

ball

all

5.

bear

ear

6.

bus

us

7.

can

an

8.

cat

at

9.

cow

ow

➡ Go to the workbook p. 2 **13**

Dd, Ee, Ff

● **Listen and repeat.** 🎧09

Dd

Ee

Ff

Ⓐ **Point and chant.** 🎧10

Dd Ee Ff

B Say and trace.

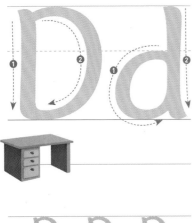
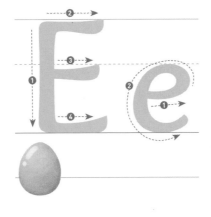
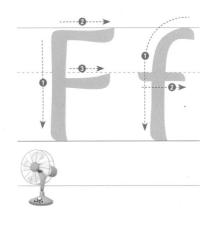

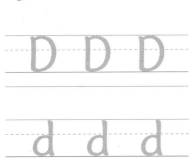

D D D   E E E   F F F

d d d   e e e   f f f

C Circle and match.

1.

D

d
a
b

2.

E

c
e
a

3.

F

f
c
e

A Listen and color. 🎧11

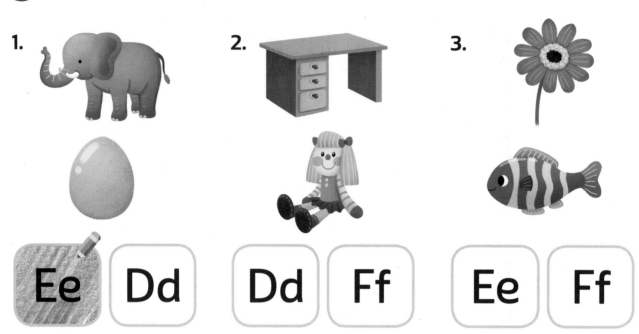

1.
Ee Dd

2.
Dd Ff

3.
Ee Ff

B Read and circle.

1.
Dd

2.
Ee

3.
Ff

C Listen, stick and read. 🎧 12

1. D

desk

dog

doll

2. E

sticker

elbow

egg

elephant

3. F

flower

sticker

fish

fan

d

e

f

Let's read together. 🎧13

I have a doll.

I have an egg.

I have a flower.

Thank you, fan!

Sight Words

have   a   an   thank   you

● **Listen and write.** 🎧 14

1.

desk

esk

2.

dog

og

3.

doll

oll

4.

egg

gg

5.

elbow

lbow

6.

elephant

lephant

7.

fan

an

8.

fish

ish

9.

flower

lower

➡ Go to the workbook p. 6 **19**

Gg, Hh, Ii

● **Listen and repeat.** 15

| Gg |  |  |  |

| Hh |  |  |  |

| Ii |  |  |  |

A **Point and chant.** 16

Gg Hh Ii

B Say and trace.

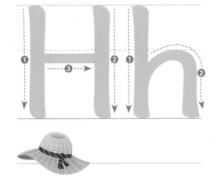
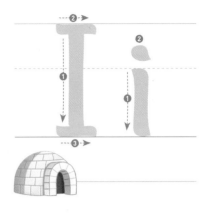

G G G

H H H

I I I

g g g

h h h

i i i

C Circle and match.

1.
G
c
g
e

2.
H
f
i
h

3.
I
i
b
h

A Listen and color.

1.

Hh   Ii

2.

Gg   Ii

3.

Hh   Gg

B Look and stick.

1.

sticker

2.

sticker

3.

sticker

4.

sticker

5.

sticker

Listen, connect and read.

1. **G**

2. **H**

3. **I**

gold

igloo

hat

house

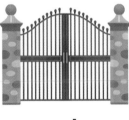

gate

iguana

ink

horse

goat

 i

g

h

Let's read together. (19)

Oh, it's a hat.

Iguana,
is this your hat?

Goat,
is this your hat?

Thank you, horse.

Sight Words

it's   is   this   your

Writing Time

● **Listen and write.** 🎧20

1.

gate

ate

2.

goat

oat

3.

gold

old

4.

hat

at

5.

horse

orse

6.

house

ouse

7.

igloo

gloo

8.

iguana

guana

9.

ink

nk

➡ Go to the workbook p. 10 **25**

Jj, Kk, Ll

● **Listen and repeat.** 21

Jj			
Kk			
Ll			

A **Point and chant.** 22

Jj   Kk   Ll

B Say and trace.

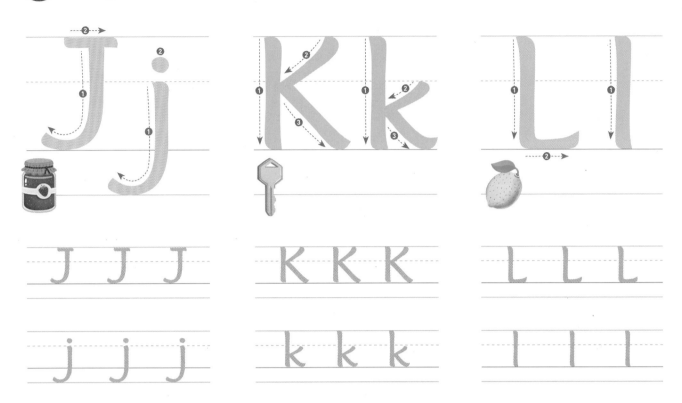

J J J

K K K

L L L

j j j

k k k

l l l

C Circle and match.

1.

J

j

i

l

2.

K

h

k

j

3.

L

i

j

l

A Listen and color. 🎧23

1.
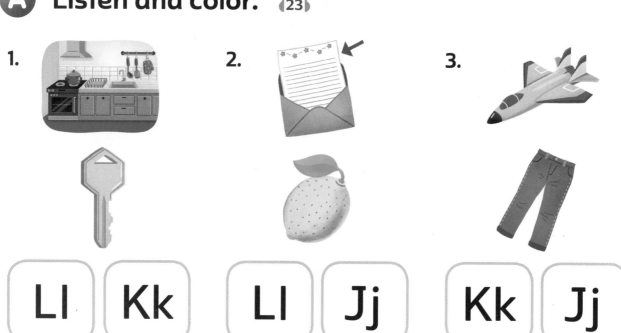

| Ll | Kk | Ll | Jj | Kk | Jj |

B Read and circle.

C **Listen, stick and read.** 🎧 24

1. **J**

jet

sticker

jeans

jam

j

2. **K**

king

sticker

key

kitchen

k

3. **L**

sticker

lemon

lion

letter

l

Story Time

● **Let's read together.** 🎧25

The lemon sees a jet.

The lemon sees a lion.

The lemon sees a key.

The lemon sees jam.

Sight Words

the　sees　a

● **Listen and write.** 🎧 26

1.

jam

am

2.

jeans

eans

3.

jet

et

4.

key

ey

5.

king

ing

6.

kitchen

itchen

7.

lemon

emon

8.

letter

etter

9.

lion

ion

A Look and match.

1.

2.

3.

A B C D E F

4.

5.

6.

B Listen and circle. 27

1. Cc (Ee) Aa

2. Ee Ff Bb

3. Bb Dd Ff

4. Cc Aa Dd

C Listen, match and write. 🎧28

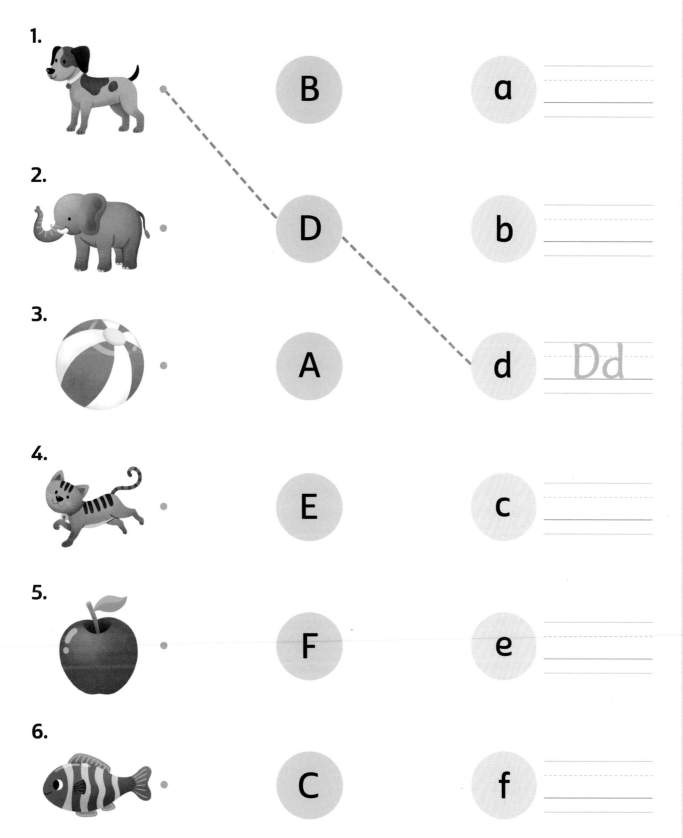

1.

B   a

2.

D   b

3.

A   d   *Dd*

4.

E   c

5.

F   e

6.

C   f

D Look and match.

1.

2.

3.

G   H   I   J   K   L

4.

5.

6.

E Listen and circle. 🎧29

1. Ii Kk Gg

2. Ll Jj Hh

3. Ii Hh Jj

4. Kk Gg Ll

F Listen, match and write. 🎧30

1.
 •   J   k _____

2.
 •   K   j _____

3.
 •   L   g _____

4.
 •   H   i _____

5.
 •   G   l _____

6.
 •   I   h _____

Mm, Nn, Oo

● **Listen and repeat.** (31)

Mm			
Nn			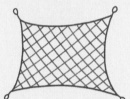
Oo			

Ⓐ **Point and chant.** (32)

Mm Nn Oo

B **Say and trace.**

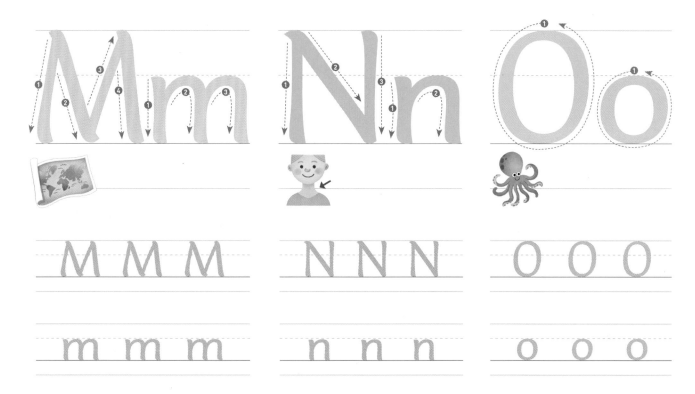

M M M

m m m

N N N

n n n

O O O

o o o

C **Circle and match.**

1.
M   o   m   n

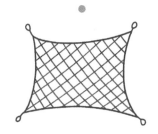

2.
N   n   k   m

3.
O   c   a   o

A Listen and color.  33

1.

2.

3.

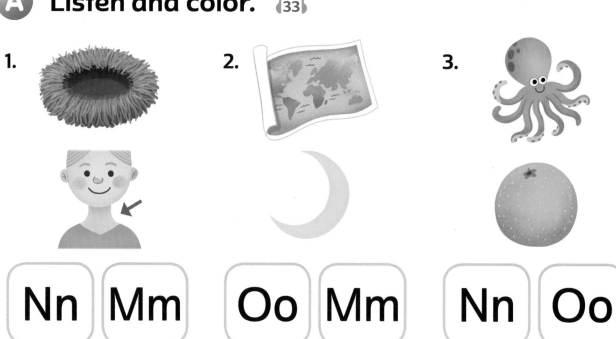

| Nn | Mm | | Oo | Mm | | Nn | Oo |

B Look and stick.

1.

sticker

2.

sticker

3.

sticker

4.

sticker

5.

sticker

Listen, connect and read.

1. **M**

2. **N**

3. **O**

moon

nest

orange

ox

monkey

neck

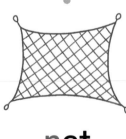

net

octopus

map

n

m

o

● **Let's read together.**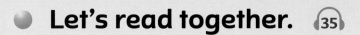

Writing Time

● **Listen and write.** 🎧36

1.

map

ap

2.

monkey

onkey

3.

moon

oon

4.

neck

eck

5.

nest

est

6.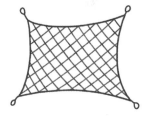

net

et

7.

octopus

ctopus

8.

orange

range

9.

ox

x

➡ Go to the workbook p. 20 **41**

Pp, Qq, Rr

Listen and repeat. 🎧37

Pp	
Qq	
Rr	

A Point and chant. 🎧38

Pp Qq Rr

B Say and trace.

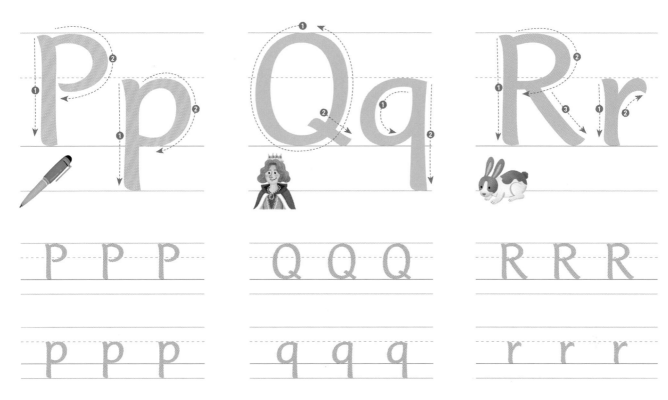

P P P

Q Q Q

R R R

p p p

q q q

r r r

C Circle and match.

1.
P
b
q
p

2.
Q
q
b
p

3.
R
p
r
q

A Listen and color. 🎧39

1.

Rr   Pp

2.

Pp   Qq

3.

Rr   Qq

B Read and circle.

1. Pp

2. Qq

3. Rr

C Listen, stick and read. 🎧40

1. P

pink

sticker

pig

pen

2. Q

question

quiet

sticker

queen

3. R

sticker

rabbit

red

ring

p q r

Let's read together. 41

The red pig is a queen.

The rabbit sees the pig.

The rabbit has a ring.

They are pink!

Sight Words

is   has   they   are

● **Listen and write.** 42

1.

pen

en

2.

pig

ig

3.

pink

ink

4.

queen

ueen

5.

question

uestion

6.

quiet

uiet

7.

rabbit

abbit

8.

red

ed

9.

ring

ing

→ Go to the workbook p. 24

Ss, Tt, Uu, Vv

● **Listen and repeat.** 43

Ss			
Tt			
Uu			
Vv			

A **Point and chant.** 44

Ss Tt Uu Vv

B Say and trace.

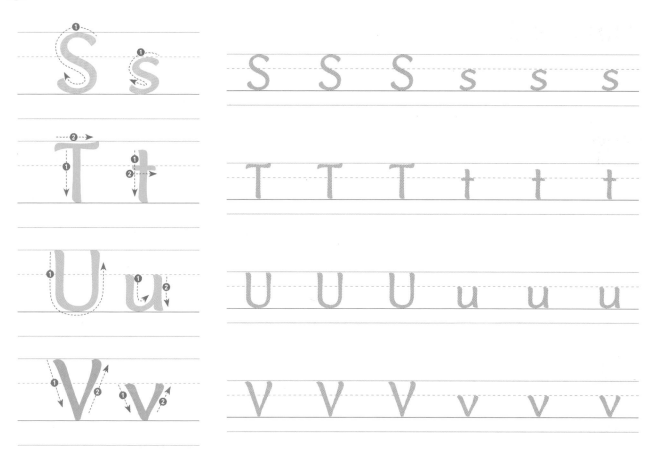

C Listen and match. 45

1. Ss
2. Tt
3. Uu
4. Vv

Listen and color. 46

1.
2.
3.
4.

Ss	Tt	Vv	Ss
Uu	Vv	Uu	Vv

Look and stick.

1. sticker
2. sticker
3. sticker

4. sticker
5. sticker
6. sticker

C **Listen, connect and read.**  🎧47

1. **S** 2. **T** 3. **U** 4. **V**

sun

umbrella

tiger

van

up

sea

vest

tail

uncle

vase

six

table

u   **s**   **v**   **t**

Let's read together. 48

The umbrella is at the sea.

The tiger is in the sea.

His uncle has a vest.

Thank you, Uncle!

Sight Words

at   in   his   has

Writing Time

Listen and write. 49

1.

sea

ea

2.

six

ix

3.

sun

un

4.

table

able

5.

tail

ail

6.

tiger

iger

7.

umbrella

mbrella

8.

uncle

ncle

9.

up

p

10.

van

an

11.

vase

ase

12.

vest

est

Ww, Xx, Yy, Zz

● **Listen and repeat.** 50

Ww			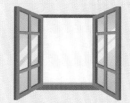
Xx			
Yy			
Zz			

A **Point and chant.** 51

Ww Xx Yy Zz

B **Say and trace.**

C **Listen and match.** 52

1. **Ww**

2. **Xx**

3. **Yy**

4. **Zz**

A Listen and color. 🎧53

1. Zz / Yy

2. Xx / Ww

3. Xx / Zz

4. Ww / Yy

B Read and circle.

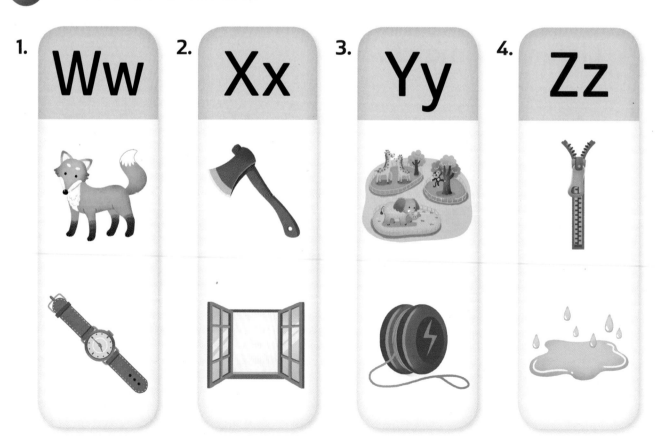

1. Ww

2. Xx

3. Yy

4. Zz

C Listen, stick and read. 54

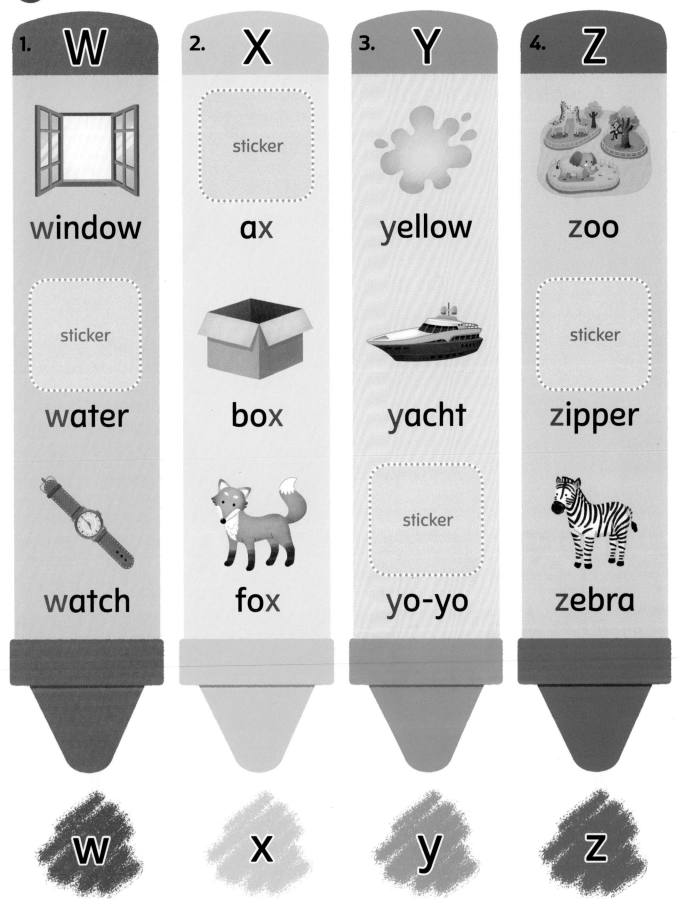

1. **W** window / water / watch
2. **X** sticker — ax / box / fox
3. **Y** yellow / yacht / yo-yo
4. **Z** zoo / zipper / zebra

w x y z

Let's read together. 55

A watch is in the box.

An ax is in the box.

A yo-yo is in the box.

A zebra is in the box.

Sight Words

is   in   the

● **Listen and write.** 56

1.

watch

atch

2.

water

ater

3.

window

indow

4.

ax

a

5.

box

bo

6.

fox

fo

7.

yacht

acht

8.

yellow

ellow

9.

yo-yo

o-yo

10.

zebra

ebra

11.

zipper

ipper

12.

zoo

oo

A Look and match.

1.
2.
3.

M　N　O　P　Q　R

4.
5.
6.

B Listen and circle. 57

1.
Oo　Pp　(Rr)

2.
Rr　Nn　Mm

3.
Mm　Qq　Oo

4.
Nn　Qq　Pp

C Listen, match and write. 🎧58

1.

O   p _____

2.

M   o _____

3.

R   n _____

4.

P   r   *Rr* _____

5.

N   m _____

6.

Q   q _____

D Look and match.

1.
2.
3.
4.

S T U V W X Y Z

5.
6.
7.
8.

E Listen and circle. 59

1. Uu Ww Yy

2. Tt Vv Uu

3. Yy Ss Zz

4. Xx Ss Vv

F Listen, write and match.

1.

Zz

2.

3.

4.

 a

 b

 c

 d

 e

 f

 g

 h

5.

6.

7.

8.

Ff, Vv / Pp, Bb / Tt, Dd

● **Listen and repeat.** 61

Ff

farm

fire

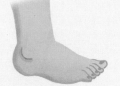

foot

Vv

van

vest

vet

A **Listen and stick.** 62

1.

Ff

2.

sticker

3.

sticker

4.

sticker

B Look and match.

1.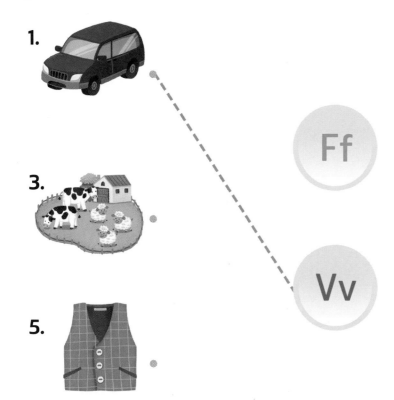

2.

Ff

3.

4.

Vv

5.

6.

C Listen and write. 🎧63

1.

farm

2.

___est

3.

___an

4.

___et

5.

___ire

6.

___oot

● **Listen and repeat.** 64

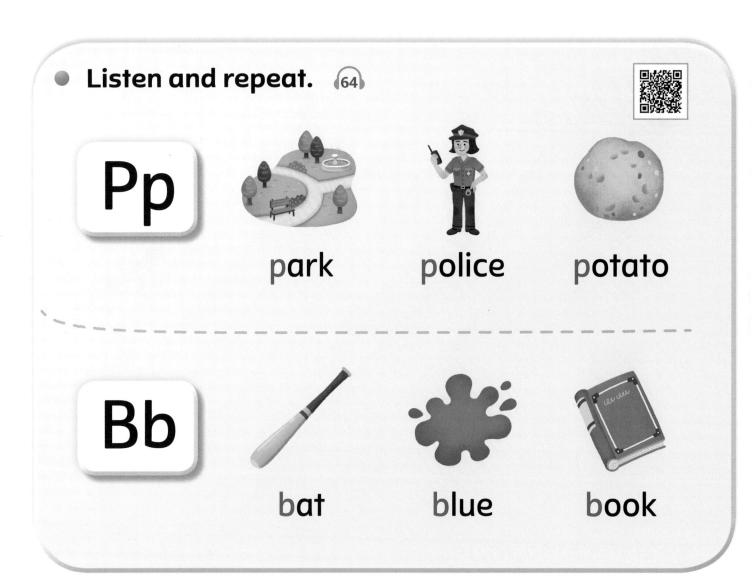

Pp — park   police   potato

Bb — bat   blue   book

A **Listen and stick.** 65

1. sticker

2. sticker

3. sticker

4. sticker

B Look and match.

1.

2.

Pp

3. 4.

Bb

5. 6.

C Listen and write. (66)

1.
at

2.
olice

3.
ark

4.
lue

5.
otato

6.
ook

● **Listen and repeat.** 🎧67

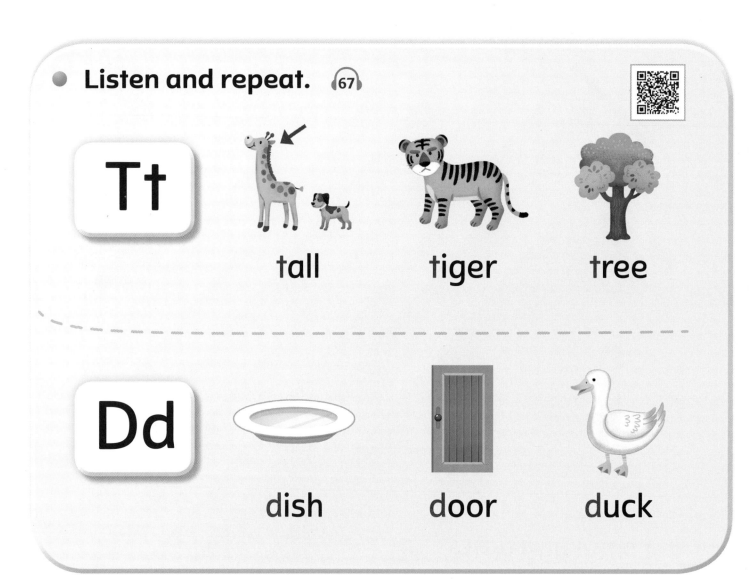

Tt

tall   tiger   tree

Dd

dish   door   duck

Ⓐ **Listen and stick.** 🎧68

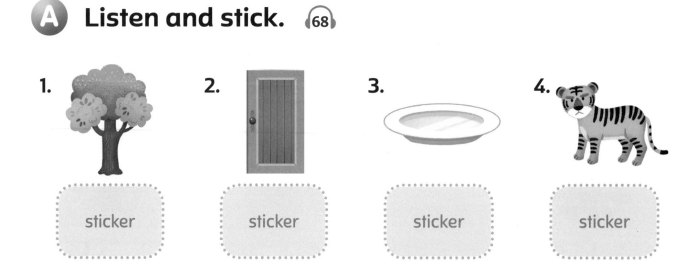

1.   2.   3.   4.

sticker   sticker   sticker   sticker

B Look and match.

1.

2.

Tt

3.

4.

Dd

5.

6.

C Listen and write. 69

1.

uck

2.

ree

3.

iger

4.

ish

5.

oor

6.

all

Ll, Rr / Mm, Nn / Ss, Zz

● **Listen and repeat.** 70

Ll

lion

long

love

Rr

rabbit

rainbow

ring

A **Listen and stick.** 71

1.

Rr

2.

sticker

3.

sticker

4.

sticker

B **Look and match.**

1.

2.

Ll

3.

4.

Rr

5.

6.

C **Listen and write.** 🎧72

1.
_ion

2.
_ong

3.
_abbit

4.
_ainbow

5.
_ove

6.
_ing

Listen and repeat. 🎧73

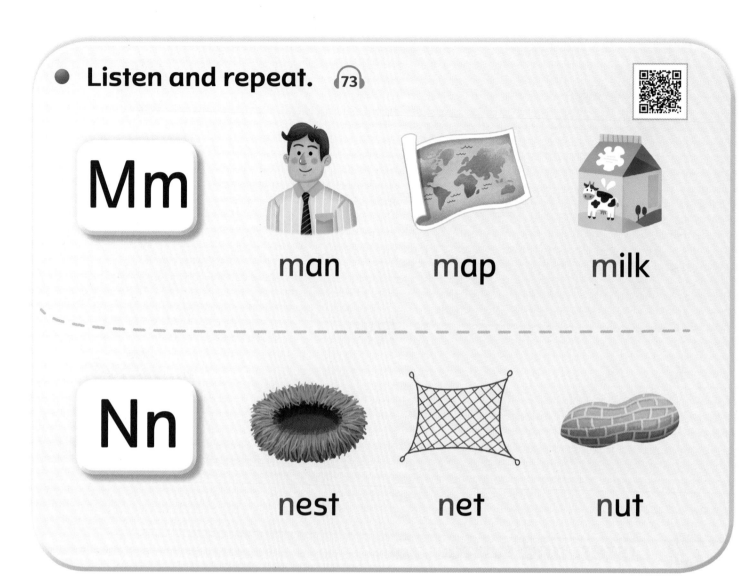

Mm

man   map   milk

Nn

nest   net   nut

A Listen and stick. 🎧74

1.

2.

3.

4.

sticker   sticker   sticker   sticker

B **Look and match.**

1.

2.

Mm

3.

4.

Nn

5.

6.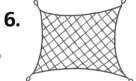

C **Listen and write.** 75

1.

ap

2.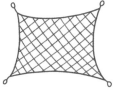

et

3.

ilk

4.

ut

5.

an

6.

est

● **Listen and repeat.** 76

Ss

sad sock stone

Zz

zebra zipper zoo

A **Listen and stick.** 77

1.

sticker

2.

sticker

3.

sticker

4.

sticker

B Look and match.

1.  •

2.  •

Ss

3.  •

4. •

Zz

5.  •

6.  •

C Listen and write. 78

1.

ock

2.

ipper

3.

oo

4.

tone

5.

ad

6.

ebra

➡ Go to the workbook p. 42 **75**

Phonics Words

Unit 01	**Aa**	alligator ☐		ant ☐		apple ☐		
	Bb	ball ☐		bear ☐		bus ☐		
	Cc	can ☐		cat ☐		cow ☐		
Unit 02	**Dd**	desk ☐		dog ☐		doll ☐		
	Ee	egg ☐		elbow ☐		elephant ☐		
	Ff	fan ☐		fish ☐		flower ☐		
Unit 03	**Gg**	gate ☐		goat ☐		gold ☐		
	Hh	hat ☐		horse ☐		house ☐		
	Ii	igloo ☐		iguana ☐		ink ☐		

Unit 04	**Jj**	jam ☐	jeans ☐	jet ☐
	Kk	key ☐	king ☐	kitchen ☐
	Ll	lemon ☐	letter ☐	lion ☐
Unit 05	**Mm**	map ☐	monkey ☐	moon ☐
	Nn	neck ☐	nest ☐	net ☐
	Oo	octopus ☐	orange ☐	ox ☐
Unit 06	**Pp**	pen ☐	pig ☐	pink ☐
	Qq	queen ☐	question ☐	quiet ☐
	Rr	rabbit ☐	red ☐	ring ☐

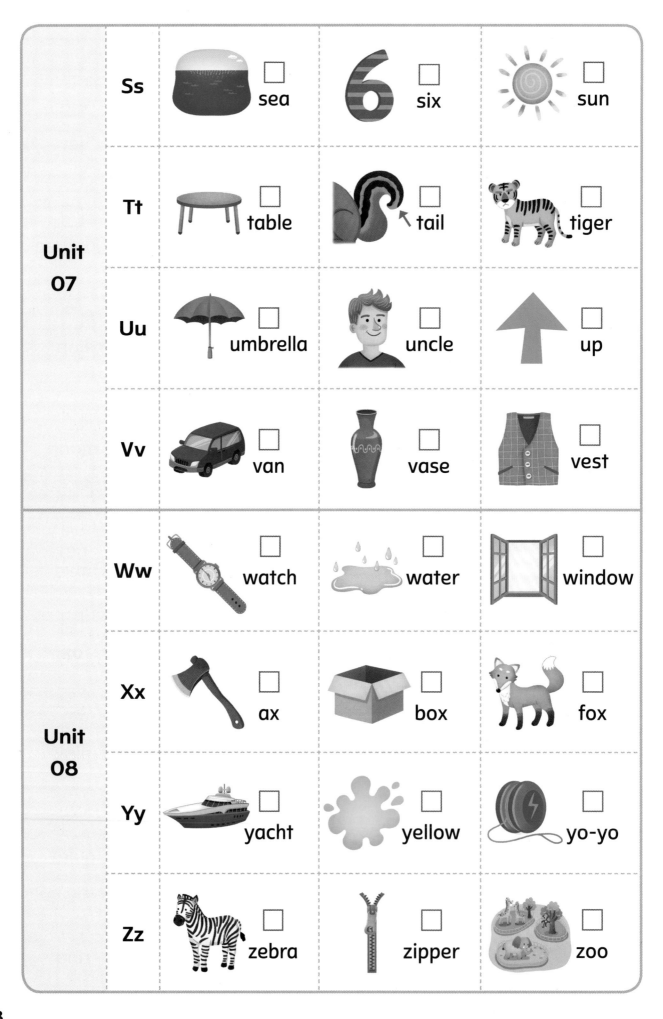

	Ss	sea ☐	six ☐	sun ☐
Unit 07	Tt	table ☐	tail ☐	tiger ☐
	Uu	umbrella ☐	uncle ☐	up ☐
	Vv	van ☐	vase ☐	vest ☐
Unit 08	Ww	watch ☐	water ☐	window ☐
	Xx	ax ☐	box ☐	fox ☐
	Yy	yacht ☐	yellow ☐	yo-yo ☐
	Zz	zebra ☐	zipper ☐	zoo ☐

Unit 09	**Ff**	☐ farm		☐ fire		☐ foot
	Vv	☐ van		☐ vest		☐ vet
	Pp	☐ park		☐ police		☐ potato
	Bb	☐ bat		☐ blue		☐ book
	Tt	☐ tall		☐ tiger		☐ tree
	Dd	☐ dish		☐ door		☐ duck
Unit 10	**Ll**	☐ lion		☐ long		☐ love
	Rr	☐ rabbit		☐ rainbow		☐ ring
	Mm	☐ man		☐ map		☐ milk
	Nn	☐ nest		☐ net		☐ nut
	Ss	☐ sad		☐ sock		☐ stone
	Zz	☐ zebra		☐ zipper		☐ zoo

• Sight Words

Unit 01	I'm	on	the	in	
Unit 02	have	a	an	thank	you
Unit 03	it's	is	this	your	
Unit 04	the	sees	a		
Unit 05	I	can	do	have	
Unit 06	is	has	they	are	
Unit 07	at	in	his	has	
Unit 08	is	in	the		

Let's Go to the English World
Phonics

Readers 1

I Like It!

 I like my alligator.

 I like gold.

 I like my bus.

 I like my hat.

 I like my fan.

Be Quiet!

The octopus is
in the kitchen.

 The pig is on the  net.

The monkey is in the jet.

 The rabbit is on the moon.

"Be quiet!"

Open the Box!

There is a **zipper** on the **box**.

Let's open the box.

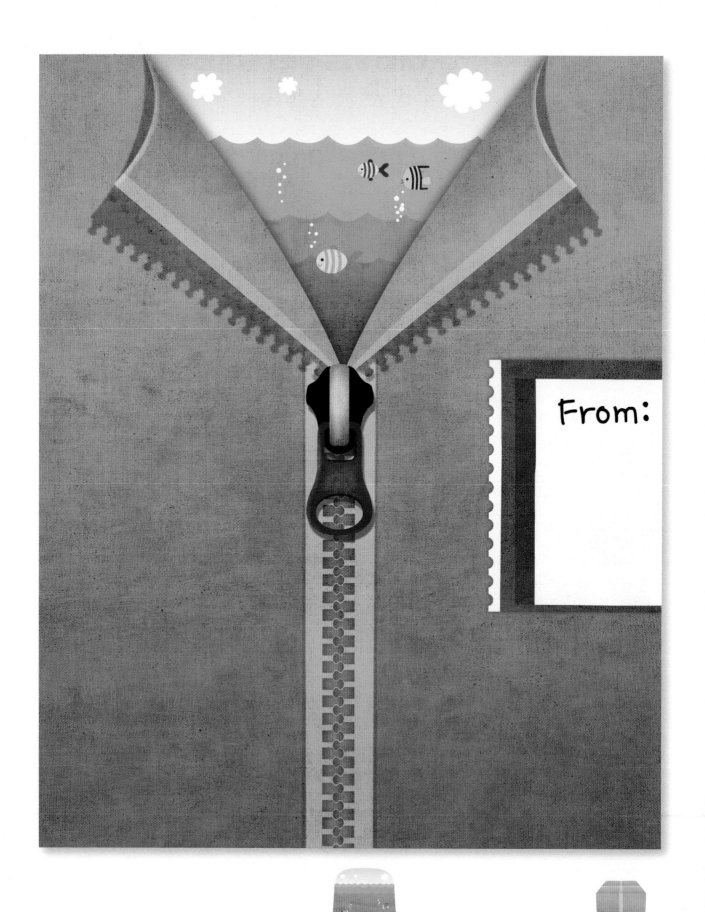

There is the sea in the box.

 There is a yacht at sea.

Oh, there is my uncle!

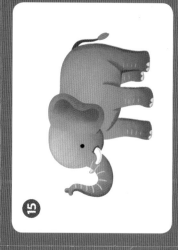

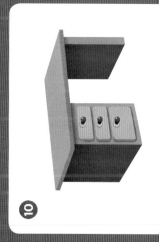

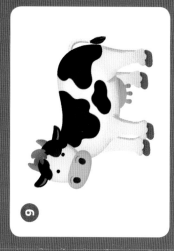

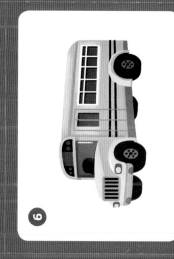

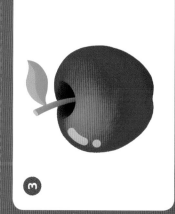

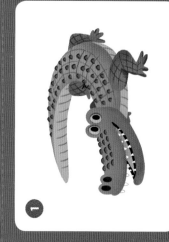

ball	cat	doll	fan
apple	can	dog	elephant
ant	bus	desk	elbow
alligator	bear	cow	egg

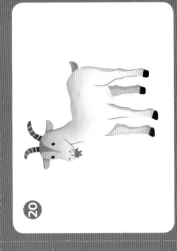

20

24

28

32

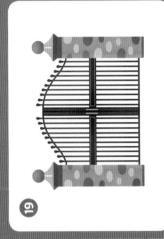

19

23

27

31

18

22

26

30

17

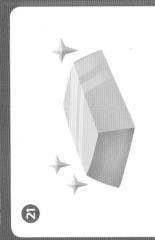

21

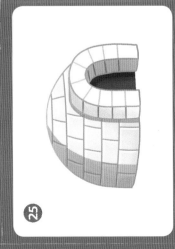

25

29

goat	house	jam	king
gate	horse	ink	key
flower	hat	iguana	jet
fish	gold	igloo	jeans

36

40

44

48

35

39

43

47

34

38

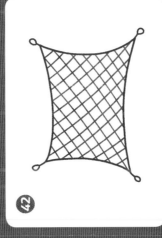

42

46

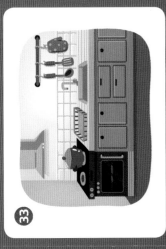

33

37

41

45

lion	neck	orange	pink
letter	moon	octopus	pig
lemon	monkey	net	pen
kitchen	map	nest	ox

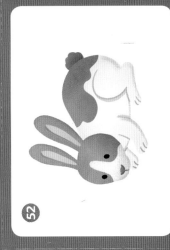

52

56

60

64

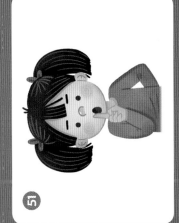

51

55

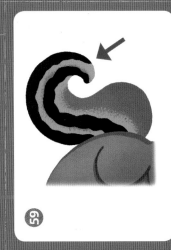

59

63

50

54

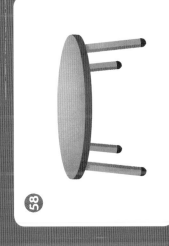

58

62

49

53

57

61

van	tiger	six	rabbit
up	tail	sea	quiet
uncle	table	ring	question
umbrella	sun	red	queen

68

72

76

80

67

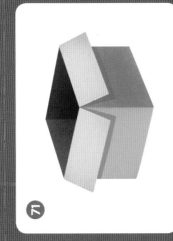

71

75

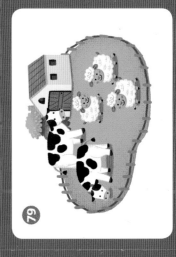

79

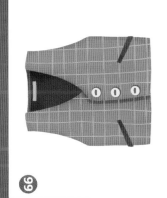

66

70

74

78

65

69

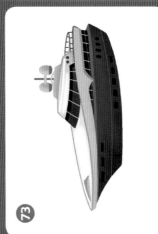

73

77

water	fox	zebra	fire
watch	box	yo-yo	farm
vest	ax	yellow	zoo
vase	window	yacht	zipper

84

88

92

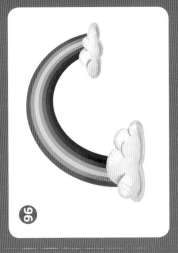

96

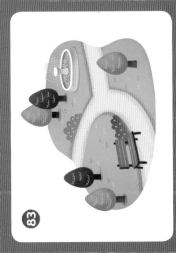

83

87

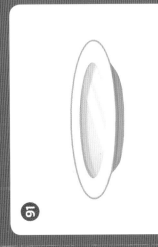

91

95

82

86

90

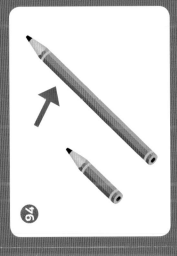

94

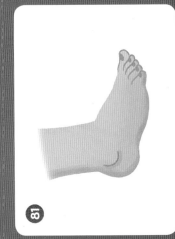

81

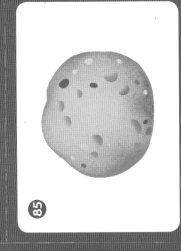

85

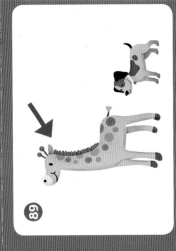

89

93

police	book	door	rainbow
park	blue	dish	love
vet	bat	tree	long
foot	potato	tall	duck

100

99

98

102

97

101

			sad
			nut
		stone	milk
		sock	man

Congratulations!

Let's Go to the English World

Phonics ❶ Single Letters

The certificate is presented to

_____ .

_____
Signature

_____
Date

Sticker Chart

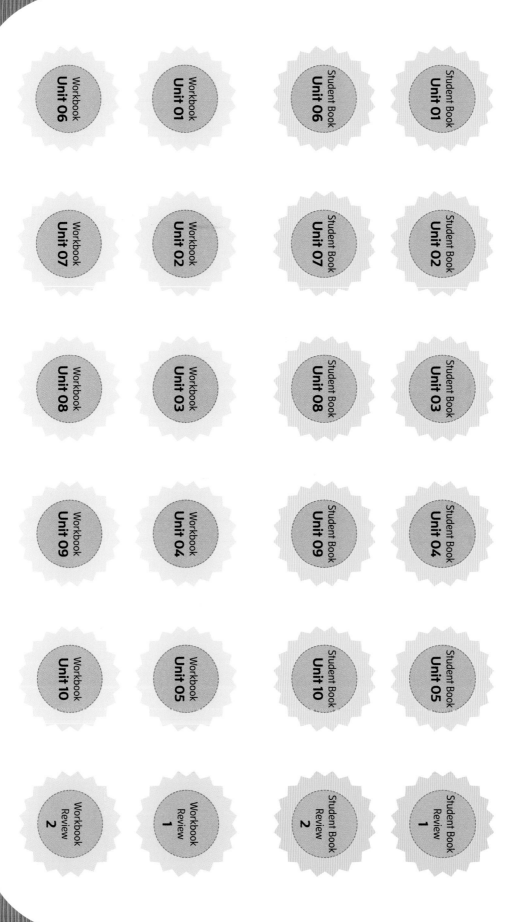

Student Book Unit 01
Student Book Unit 02
Student Book Unit 03
Student Book Unit 04
Student Book Unit 05

Student Book Unit 06
Student Book Unit 07
Student Book Unit 08
Student Book Unit 09
Student Book Unit 10

Student Book Review 1
Student Book Review 2

Workbook Unit 01
Workbook Unit 02
Workbook Unit 03
Workbook Unit 04
Workbook Unit 05

Workbook Unit 06
Workbook Unit 07
Workbook Unit 08
Workbook Unit 09
Workbook Unit 10

Workbook Review 1
Workbook Review 2

Unit 01 p. 10

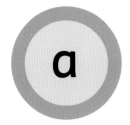 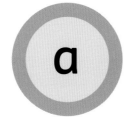 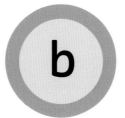 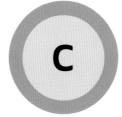

Unit 02 p. 17

Unit 03 p. 22

Unit 04 p. 29

Unit 05 p. 38

 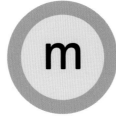   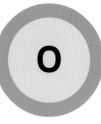

Unit 06 p. 45

Unit 07 p. 50

| s | t | u | u | v | v |

Unit 08 p. 57

Unit 09

p. 64

| Ff | Vv | Vv |

p. 66

| Pp | Pp | Bb | Bb |

p. 68

| Tt | Tt | Dd | Dd |

Unit 10

p. 70

| Ll | Ll | Rr |

p. 72

| Mm | Mm | Nn | Nn |

p. 74

| Ss | Ss | Zz | Zz |

Praise Stickers

2nd Edition

LET'S GO
to the English World

1

WORKBOOK

Phonics

Single Letters

CHUNJAE EDUCATION, INC.

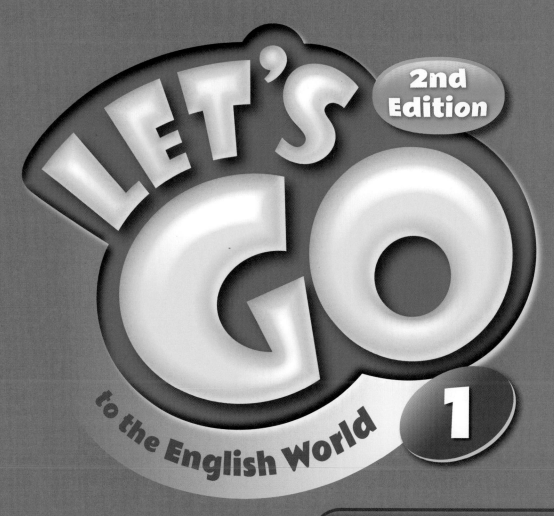

2nd Edition

LET'S GO

to the English World

1

WORKBOOK

Phonics

CHUNJAE EDUCATION, INC.

Single Letters

A Say and write.

1.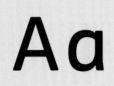

A A A A A A A

a a a a a a a

2.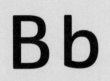

B

b

3.

C

c

B Read and color.

1.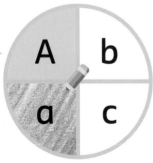

A	b
a	c

2.

C	a
b	c

3.

B	a
c	b

C Look and circle.

1.

2.

 Bb

3.

 Cc

D Say and circle.

1.

c
a
b

2.

b
a
c

3.

a
c
b

E **Look and match.**

1. A   2. B   3. C

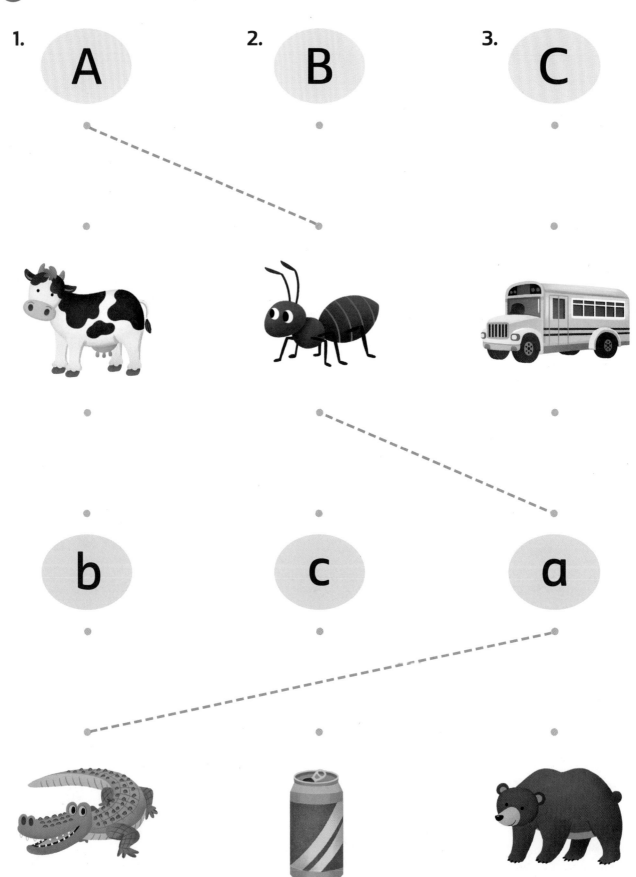

b   c   a

F Choose and write.

a   b   c

1.

___a__pple

2.

___us

3.

___ow

4.

___ear

5.

___an

6.

___nt

7.

___at

8.

___lligator

9.

___all

A Say and write.

1.
Dd

D

d

2.
Ee

E

e

3.
Ff

F

f

B Read and color.

1.

F	d
e	f

2.

D	d
f	e

3.

E	f
e	d

C Look and circle.

1.

2.

 Ee

3.

 Ff

D Say and circle.

1.
e
f
d

2.
d
f
e

3.
e
d
f

Look and match.

1. D

2. E

3. F

e

d

f

F **Choose and write.**

d   e   f

1.

___oll

2.

___lephant

3.

___lower

4.

___lbow

5.

___ish

6.

___esk

7.

___og

8.

___an

9.

___gg

Unit 03 Gg, Hh, Ii

A Say and write.

1.
Gg

G
g

2.
Hh

H
h

3.
Ii

I
i

B Read and color.

1.
G	g
h	i

2.
I	h
g	i

3.
H	i
h	g

C Look and circle.

1.

2.

3.

D Say and circle.

1.
h
g
i

2.
g
i
h

3.
i
h
g

E Look and match.

1. G

2. H

3. I

i

g

h

F **Choose and write.**

g　　h　　i

1.

__guana

2.

__ouse

3.

__oat

4.

__ate

5.

__nk

6.

__orse

7.

__at

8.

__gloo

9.

__old

A Say and write.

1.

J

j

2.

K

k

3.

L

l

B Read and color.

1.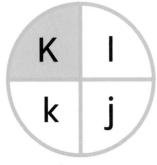

2.

3.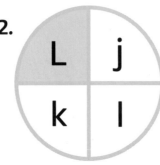

C Look and circle.

1.
 Jj

2.
 Kk

3.
 Ll

D Say and circle.

1.
l
j
k

2.
k
j
l

3.
j
l
k

E **Look and match.**

1. J

2. K

3. L

k

l

j

Choose and write.

j   k   l

1.

___am

2.

___ing

3.

___emon

4.

___ey

5.

___etter

6.

___et

7.

___eans

8.

___itchen

9.

___ion

Review 1

A Look and circle.

1. **Hh**
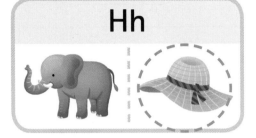

2. **Cc**
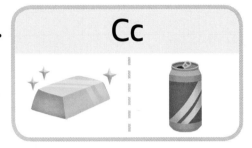

3. **Ff**

4. **Kk**
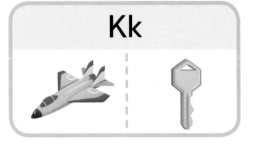

5. **Aa**
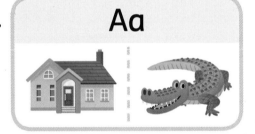

6. **Ii**
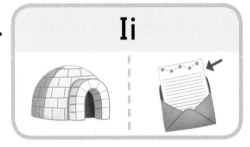

B Write and say.

1.
_e_lbow

2.
___us

3.
___emon

4.
___ate

5.
___eans

6.
___esk

C Look and write.

1.

Kk

_k_ing

___ey

2.

Dd

___og

___oll

3.

Gg

___old

___oat

4.

Cc

___at

___an

Unit 05 Mm, Nn, Oo

A Say and write.

1.

M
_____
m

2.

N
_____
n

3.

O
_____
o

B Read and color.

1.
| N | o |
| m | n |

2.
| O | m |
| n | o |

3.
| M | o |
| m | n |

C Look and circle.

1.

2.

3.

D Say and circle.

1.

m
o
n

2.

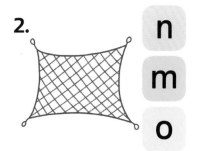

n
m
o

3.

o
n
m

E **Look and match.**

1. M   2. N   3. O

o   n   m

F Choose and write.

m　　　n　　　o

1.

__ctopus

2.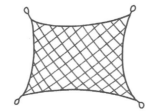

__et

3.

__ap

4.

__oon

5.

__x

6.

__eck

7.

__est

8.

__range

9.

__onkey

A Say and write.

1.
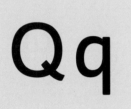

P _____

p _____

2.

Q _____

q _____

3.

R _____

r _____

B Read and color.

1.

Q	r
p	q

2.

P	q
p	r

3.

R	r
q	p

C Look and circle.

1.

2.

Qq

3.

Rr

D Say and circle.

1.

r
p
q

2.

p
q
r

3.

q
r
p

E **Look and match.**

1.
P

2.
Q

3.
R

q

p

r

F **Choose and write.**

p　　q　　r

1.

___ink

2.

___ueen

3.

___abbit

4.

___ing

5.

___en

6.

___uiet

7.

___uestion

8.

___ed

9.

___ig

A Say and write.

1.

Ss

S
_____

s
_____

2.

Tt

T
_____

t
_____

3.

Uu

U
_____

u
_____

4.

Vv

V
_____

v
_____

B Read and color.

1.
2.
3.
4.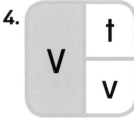

C Look and circle.

1. Ss
2. Tt
3. Uu
4. Vv

D Say and circle.

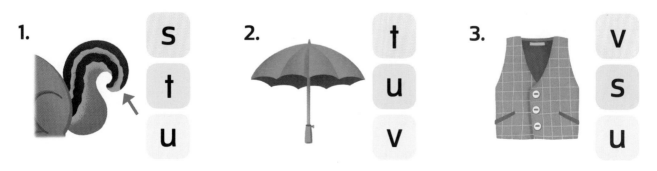

1. s / t / u
2. t / u / v
3. v / s / u

E **Look and match.**

1. **S**   2. **T**   3. **U**   4. **V**

v   **s**   **t**   **u**

F Choose and write.

s t u v

1.

____un

2.

____able

3.

____p

4.

____est

5.

____iger

6.

____an

7.

____ix

8.

____ncle

9.

____ase

10.

____ail

11.

____ea

12.

____mbrella

Unit 08 · Ww, Xx, Yy, Zz

A Say and write.

1.

W

w

2.

X

x

3.

Y

y

4.

Z

z

B Read and color.

1.
2.
3.
4.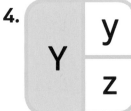

C Look and circle.

1. Ww
2. Xx
3. Yy
4. Zz

D Say and circle.

1. y / w / z
2. w / x / y
3. z / y / x

E **Look and match.**

1. W   2. X   3. Y   4. Z

w   x   z   y

F Choose and write.

W X Y Z

1. __oo

2. __atch

3. __o-yo

4. fo__

5. __indow

6. __ebra

7. __ater

8. a__

9. __ellow

10. __ipper

11. __acht

12. bo__

Review 2

A Look and circle.

1. **Zz**
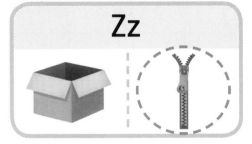

2. **Vv**
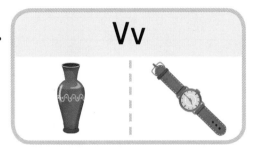

3. **Rr**
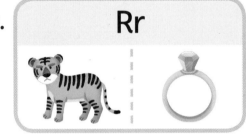

4. **Ss**

5. **Mm**

6. **Qq**

B Write and say.

1.
<u>w</u>indow

2.
__acht

3.
__ail

4.
__ap

5.
__x

6.
__ig

C Look and write.

1.

Pp

_p_ink

___en

2.

Nn

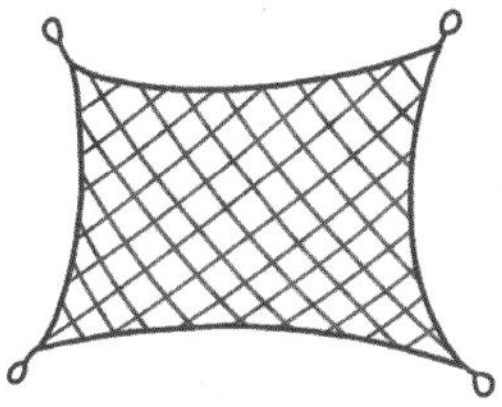

__et

__est

3.

Ss

__ix

__ea

4.

Xx

fo__

a__

A Look and circle.

1.

 Ff |

2.

 Vv |

B Say and color.

1. 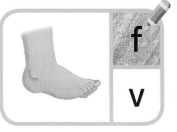 f / v

2.  f / v

3.  f / v

4.  f / v

5.  f / v

6.  f / v

C Look and circle.

1.

 Pp

2.

 Bb

D Choose and circle.

1.
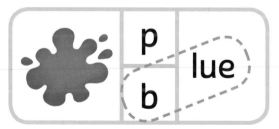

p	
b	lue

2.

p	
b	ark

3.

p	
b	olice

4.

p	
b	at

E Look and circle.

1.

2.

F Match and write.

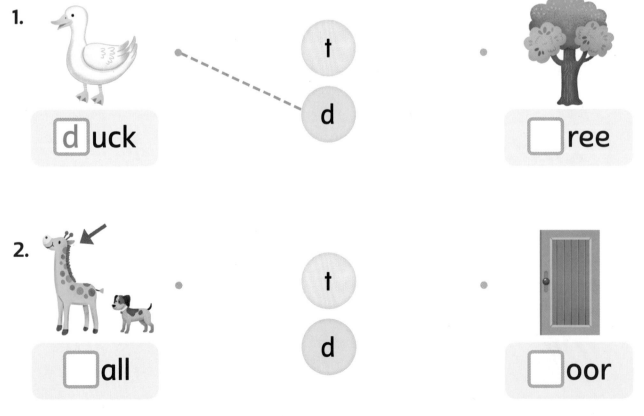

1.

d uck

t

d

ree

2.

all

t

d

oor

G Choose and write.

f   v   p   b   t   d

1.

__at

2.

__otato

3.

__uck

4.

__olice

5.

__ire

6.

__est

7.

__ree

8.

__et

9.

__ook

10.

__oot

11.

__all

12.

__ish

A Look and circle.

1.

2.

B Say and color.

1.
l
r

2.
l
r

3.
l
r

4.
l
r

5.
l
r

6.
l
r

C Look and circle.

1.

2.

 Nn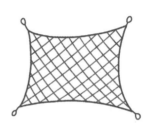

D Choose and circle.

1.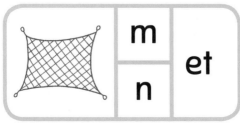
m	ut
n	

2.
m	an
n	

3.
m	et
n	

4.
m	ilk
n	

1.

 Ss

2.

 Zz

F Match and write.

1.

☐ad

S

Z

☐ipper

2.

☐ebra

S

Z

☐tone

Choose and write.

l   r   m   n   s   z

1. _____an

2. _____ut

3. _____ipper

4. _____est

5. _____ong

6. _____ainbow

7. _____ove

8. _____abbit

9. _____ock

10. _____oo

11. _____ad

12. _____ilk

Final Review

● **Choose and write.**

a b c d e f g h i

 __f__ an

 __ gloo

 __ ow

 __ ouse

 __ ear

 __ gg

 __ nk

 __ oll

 __ nt

 __ ate

 __ at

 __ all

 __ oat

 __ esk

 __ ish

 __ at

j k l m n o p q r

__ion

__ing

__oon

__et

__est

__ed

__ey

__abbit

__ig

__emon

__am

__ap

__uiet

__en

__x

__eck

__ea

bo__

__ncle

__acht

__p

__an

__un

__ater

__oo

__o-yo

__atch

__iger

a__

__ail

__est

__ipper